ADDITIONAL NOTES ON ARROW RELEASE

By EDWARD S. MORSE

British Library Cataloguing-in-Publication Data
A catalogue record for this book is available from the
British Library

There is no excellence in archery without great labour.

— MAURICE THOMPSON

(*Fig. 26*) Negrito Bowmen. Philippine Islands

THE HISTORY OF ARCHERY

A GLANCE AT THE CAREER OF
THE ENGLISH LONG-BOW

by Horace A. Ford

The date of the first introduction of the long-bow into
England is a matter of considerable uncertainty, and a *cheval
de bataille* with all historians and authors who have attempted
to determine it; but it is certain that it was not till after the
battle of Hastings, and the subsequent conquest of Britain
by the Normans, that it became he favourite and specially
encouraged military weapon in the hands of its inhabitants.
The preponderance of historical evidence goes to prove that,
to the deadly effects produced by it in that battle, the invaders
principally owed their victory—Harold himself and the best
of his men falling victims to the clothyard shaft. Thus the
long-bow proved the prime agent in subjugating this country,
substituting the Norman for the Saxon rule, and, by the
intermixture of the two people, ultimately in completing that
far-famed Anglo-Saxon race, the popularly supposed powers
of which to accomplish everything everywhere it behoveth not
one of themselves further to dilate upon. From this time, then,
we may conclude, commenced in England that general, and all

but universal, cultivation of the bow, which was ultimately to lead to such marvellous and astounding results, and to render the very name of the, English bowman an object of terror and dread in the minds of his enemies. Archers we find employed on both sides in the civil contests between Stephen and Matilda, and during the reign of Henry II. they began to form the larger portion of the infantry of the English armies, and to evince that decided superiority over those of every other nation which they ever afterwards retained.

In this reign, too, first appeared upon the scene that prince of good fellows (as times went) and gentlest of robbers and outlaws, bold Robin Hood!—that hero of impossible shots, the twang of whose bow, with that "of his jolly companions everyone," could, according to Drayton, be heard a mile off! *Credat Judaeus!* However this may be, if there be truth at all in history and legend, he and his merry men were incomparable Archers, for strength and skill never surpassed, if ever equalled; and we may well suppose Archery to have been brought to the highest pitch of perfection in the times that produced such eminent exemplifiers of the Art. Robin flourished much longer than is usual with such bold spirits, even in the olden time; for we find him still in his glory through the reign of Richard I, John, and a considerable portion of that of his successor, Henry III.

It would be impossible, without entering into a mass of details whose length *would* be unsuited to the nature of these pages, to mention a tithe of the extraordinary feats performed and victories gained by the English during the next three or four centuries, owing entirely to their superiority in the use of the long-bow. The fictions of romance pale before many of the authenticated tales handed down to us by historians of the wonders it achieved. No armour that could be made proved strong enough to insure its wearer against its power, no superiority of numbers seemed sufficient to wrest a victory from its grasp. Speed declares that the armour worn by Earl Douglas and his men-at-arms at the battle of Homildon had been three years in making, and was of remarkable temper, yet the "English arrows rent it with little adoe." Gibbon tells us that, on one occasion, during the Crusades, "Richard, with seventeen knights and three hundred archers, sustained the charge of the whole Turkish and Saracen army;" and the pages of Froissart teem with the details of battles and skirmishes without number, in which the irresistible power placed by it in the hands of the English enabled them to set all odds at defiance, and constantly to emerge victorious out of situations where utter destruction seemed certain and inevitable. Look at Cressy and Poictiers, Navaretta and Agincourt! Since the extinction of the bow as a weapon of war, has England ever shown parallels to such victories as these? "Let him," says Roberts, "who reads the history of modern times, look narrowly to find, if but once (since Archery flourished), with our *twelve or fifteen thousand* we have defeated an army *of fifty or sixty thousand*;" and he might have added, as was the case in the last-named battle, if with twenty-five thousand we had completely routed and nearly annihilated an army of a *hundred and sixty thousand*! And be it also borne in mind that these marvellous and wondrous results were not obtained against barbarian hordes or undisciplined soldiery, but against some of the first chivalry and most renowned men-at-arms that the world at that time contained. In spite of Miniés and breech-loading rifles, will it ever again become a proverb in vogue regarding the British soldier, that he carries as many enemies' lives in his hands as bullets in his pouch; yet it was a common saying in Scotland in times gone by, that every English Archer bore with him the lives of four-and-twenty Scots— such being the number of arrows each carried in his quiver. All honour, then, to the long-bow! May the grateful remembrance of it never pass away from the land, whose glory it has raised to so high a pitch; and though it may never be seen a weapon of war again, may its practice long continue to form one of our most manly and health-inspiring amusements.

The time that Archery commenced its decline in this country, till it finally ceased to be used in warfare at all, is almost as much a matter of dispute with writers as is the date of its first introduction. If we are to believe Moseley, "the battle of Agincourt (which happened under Henry V., 1415) is the last important action in which Archery is mentioned;" but according to Roberts, (whose accuracy in matters of historical detail can in general be well depended on,) great slaughter was caused by it in the civil wars between the White and Red Roses; and he further adds, "it continued to support its military character and invincible career of glory with undiminished effect during the reigns of Henry VI., Henry VII., Henry VIII., and Edward VI., and even in the reign of Elizabeth was still in high repute amongst foreigners of great military skill, who had witnessed its powerful effects." Nevertheless, we find Hollingshead, who wrote in the sixteenth century, bewailing the degeneracy of the Archery of his day, as being deficient in force and strength. The mean between the extremes of conflicting opinions will probably lead us to the nearest approximation to the truth. It may, therefore, be concluded that towards the close of the fifteenth century the use of fire-arms had caused Archery to be held in somewhat less repute than formerly, and that, consequently, the cultivation of it had ceased to be of that all but universal character that it once had been. The natural effects followed—with less practice came less strength and skill; and by the time the sixteenth century came to an end, but little remained to the bow, beyond the remembrance of its former glory and achievements. The last mention of Archery as used in warfare, occurs in a pamphlet published in 1664, where it is stated to have been employed in the contests between the Marquis of Montrose and the Scots; but evidently for many years prior to this date, its ancient pith, power, and reputation, had departed.

We now arrive at the time when the bow, abandoned as a weapon of war, became a mere instrument of amusement and recreation; but hardly any record exists to enlighten us as to the extent to which it was practised, or the degree of skill retained by its admirers. During the eighteenth century it would almost appear to have fallen entirely into disuse, only two or three societies existing in the kingdom, and those in a very languid and feeble condition. In the year 1780, however, a society, under the title of The Royal Toxophilites, was established in London; and, the impetus once communicated, a great revival of Archery immediately took place, and a vast number of societies speedily sprang up in every part of the country, the greater part of which, with many new and more modern ones, exist in full force and vigour at the present day. Undoubtedly, however, we owe to the establishment of the Grand National Archery Society, fourteen years back, the present high consideration in which the practice of Archery is by both sexes now held, as well as the more general and increasing skill which continues year by year plainly to manifest itself—thus showing that the love of the bow has only slumbered, not died, in the breasts of Englishmen, and needs but moderate encouragement to become once more, if not a weapon of war, at any rate one of the most esteemed and highly-prized amusements in the kingdom. To conclude, let every Briton remember, in the words of Camden, that when Englishmen used Hercules' weapons—the *bow* and the black bill—they fought victoriously, "with *Hercules' success*"—and reverence their memory accordingly.

Essay taken from *Archery, its Theory and Practice* by Horace A. Ford originally published 1859.

ADDITIONAL NOTES ON ARROW RELEASE

Edward S. Morse

In 1885 I published, in the *Proceedings of the Essex Institute*, a paper entitled "Ancient and Modern Methods of Arrow Release." From the difficulty I found in ascertaining the various attitudes of the hand in drawing the bow I began to realize that no one had made a study of the subject and that I had made a discovery. Prof. E. B. Tylor, the distinguised author of "Prehistoric Times," in acknowledging the receipt of a copy of my paper, wrote me as follows: "It is wonderful how much there is to be learned by close examination into points that at first sight do not seem as if they wanted any. I had no idea till I looked at your sketches that there were systematic differences among peoples in their way of discharging their arrows."* The main facts, with their illustrations, quickly appeared in Russian, German, Dutch and French reviews and were republished in England and started a number of investigators on the subject. In the Memoir, which has been out of print for some years I asked for information on the subject particularly concerning savage people, as I regarded my work as only a preliminary outline of the subject. As a result of this appeal

---

*In the Badminton Library. Archery, C. J. Longman, Esq., says (p. 76) "In discussing methods of drawing the bow occasion will ·frequently arise to refer to the pamphlet by Prof. Morse, as he was the first to investigate the subject. His researches on a seemingly trivial matter have a high ethnographic interest, and his classification is so sound that it must form the basis of any further researches on the subject."

1

I received many items and sketches from all parts of the world and now, nearly thirty-five years after, I have compiled this information and the present paper is the result.

Before proceeding further I venture at this point to republish a few figures illustrating the five forms of arrow release† given in my first paper on the subject which has long been out of print.

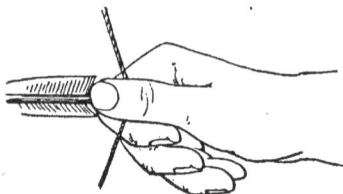

PRIMARY RELEASE

Fig. 1

I found the simplest form of release was that which the children of all nations use the world over: that is in grasping the arrow with the thumb and bent forefinger. I have seen the children of Americans, Indians, Chinese, Japanese and Negroes play with a toy bow and arrow and they all invariably grasp the arrow with the thumb and bent forefinger. It was interesting to discover that some of the lower savage races, like the Ainu, practice this release. The arrow accompanying this release is generally knobbed at the nock end and is gashed or roughened to secure a firmer pinch on the arrow. This I termed the primary release.

---

†The English archer prefers the word "loose" to release. Release seems to me better word for we release a prisoner; we speak of a loose button, a loose hinge, something that is still there, like a loose tooth.

2

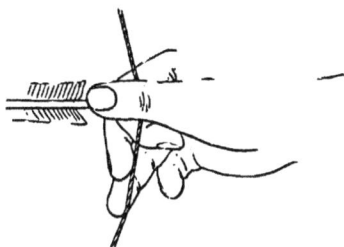

SECONDARY RELEASE
Fig. 2

In another and higher group of savages such as the Pueblo Indians, the arrow is not only grasped by the thumb and bent forefinger but the second and third fingers are brought to bear upon the string, thus enabling the archer to use a stronger bow. This I termed the secondary release.

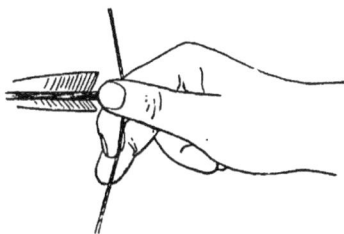

TERTIARY RELEASE
Fig. 3

A third form of release I determined through the courtesy of MR. LE FLESCHE, an educated Omaha Indian. This release consisted in holding the forefinger nearly straight and not bent as in the primary and secondary releases and with the tips of this finger and the tips of the second and third fingers pulling the string, the arrow being held between the tips of the thumb and forefinger. This

3

form I termed the tertiary release and found it wide spread. From the testimony of LIEUT. VOGDES, U. S. A. and COL. JAMES STEPHENSON, this was the form of release used by the Sioux, Arapahoes,. Cheyennes, Assiniboins, Comanches, Blackfeet and Navahoes and doubtless other North American tribes.

C. J. LONGMAN, Esq., in his interesting and valuable contributions to the Archery volume of the *Badminton Library Series*, does not recognize this release and classifies it with the secondary form and says, "It seems doubtful, however whether there is sufficient distinction between the secondary and tertiary looses to justify their separation, and all finger and thumb looses, when the tips of the fingers assist in drawing the string will be classed here as secondary." I cannot agree with my distinguished friend, for further study shows that it is a marked North American method. A study of West Coast Indians, Mexican tribes, Surinam Indians, and even the figures in ancient Mexican codices, tracings of which I have received from that eminent scholar MRS. ZELIA NUTTALL, convinces me that the tertiary release was employed by these ancient people. It is found sporadically in other parts of the world.

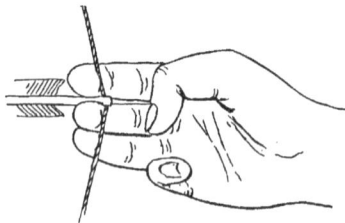

MEDITERRANEAN RELEASE
Fig. 4

The archers of Europe shooting only for sport use a release that I have named the Mediterranean release because I discovered that

4

the Mediterranean nations - the Caucasians of Blumenbach - for nearly 2000 years have used this release.* Even the ancient relatives of this race, the Hill tribes of India, practice it. It consists in drawing the string with the tips of the first, second and third fingers; the thumb is inert and the little finger is rarely used. Pictures and engravings of the 17th century and before depict the archer as using the first and second finger only. This indicates either greater strength or a lighter bow. This release, as practiced today requires either a glove or finger tips of leather to protect the ends of the fingers.

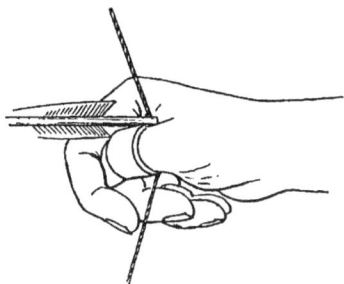

MONGOLIAN RELEASE
Fig. 5

The Asiatic races employ a method far removed from those forms already mentioned. The string is drawn back by the thumb which is sharply bent over it, while the forefinger is bent over the tip of the thumb to aid in holding it. The arrow is held in the junction of the forefinger and thumb. This method of release necessitates

*HAROLD H. BENDER, Professor of Indo-Germanic Philology at Princeton University has lately published an extremely illuminating book, entitled "The Home of the Indo-European." He gives good reasons for believing that the term Indo-European is preferable to that of Aryan or Mediterranean. The term Caucasian of Blumenbach is, of course, nearly obsolete.

the wearing of a stout thumb-ring made of bone, horn, jade or metal, the edge of the ring engaging the string. All the Asiatic races without exception use this realese; the Mongols, Manchus, Tibetans, Koreans and Turks use this release with various forms of thumb rings, the Japanese using a glove with a grooved thumb. Even the Persians, who are not Mongoloid, have acquired this release from being interposed between Mongoloid people on the east and west.

In attempting to make out from ancient drawings, such as those on Greek vases, the attitude of the hand in drawing the bow the great difficulty arises from the fact that in many cases the artist was not an archer, and, furthermore, so long as the bow was stretched no attention was paid to the attitude of the hand in stretching it. When I began the study I was amazed at the inability of travelers to recall the method of arrow release, though they admitted they had seen the savages shoot a hundred times. I recall a striking illustration of this in the case of my friend, FRANK HAMILTON CUSHING, who had lived among the Zuni Indians for several years. He brought to Boston many years ago a number of Zuni Indians who were hospitably entertained by MRS. MARY HEMENWAY at her summer home in Manchester. I was invited to spend the day with them. I asked MR. CUSHING the method the Zuni used in shooting the arrow. He looked at me vaguely and said, "Why, I have shot with them a thousand times, isn't it this way?" pushing a lead pencil between the thumb and bent forefinger. I told him that was the lowest form of release and as the Zuni are Pueblo Indians I thought they must use the secondary release, that is beside the thumb and bent forefinger on the arrow, the second and third finger assisted in drawing the string. He immediately constructed a bow from a stick, made a rude arrow, strung the stick and invited one of the chiefs to illustrate the Zuni method of drawing the bow. We eagerly watched the hand as he drew the string and the attitude of his fingers was precisely as I had predicted. MR. CUSHING gave me a hearty slap on the shoulder while ejaculating "Spl — endid!" Now here was an acute observer who had lived and shot with the Zuni and yet had failed to observe the simple atti-

6

tude of the hand in shooting. What must it have been with the ancient artists and sculptors, many of whom had never shot an arrow! The infinite variety of drawings on Greek vases of archers drawing the bow is sufficient evidence of their incompetency in regard to portraying the attitude of the hand in archery. In ancient rock sculpture the wear and tear of age render the details indistinct, the position of the fingers on the bow string is often obscure. These conditions coupled with the inaccuracy of the sculptor render these details unreliable. The general attitude of the hand, however, can be recognized. In all the releases except the Mongolian the attitude of the hand as a whole can usually be seen and it assumes the form of a more or less closed fist. In the Mongolian release, however, the attitude of the hand is with fingers bending downward at right angles to the back of the hand which is uppermost.

In my first memoir I expressed the belief that the different releases characterized different races and that is more or less true. I find that these lines are not hard and fast, however, as I had at first supposed but that here and there savage people the world over practice a release which I associated with the higher races, namely, the Mediterranean. Even the Mongolian release, the most exclusive of them all, is found in Africa in which not only the thumb-ring is used but also an extraordinary device in the form of a yoke of wood grasped in the hand and first described by DR. FELIX VON LUSCHAN. Further reference to his discovery will be made.

In my first paper I tried in vain to find the method of release among the Indians who were common in New England in the early part of the seventeenth century. I had secured the Penobscot and Micmac release and this was the primary form. In 1865 the Prince Society of Boston reproduced a rare book entitled "Wood's New-England's Prospect," by WILLIAM WOOD, published in London in 1634, copies of which are of great rarity. In the Prince Society reproduction the quaint and original spelling is carefully preserved. WILLIAM WOOD was evidently a gentleman and a scholar, Latin phrases often occur. The author was a keen observer. He notices what few travelers do,

7

the attitude of the hand of the savage in drawing the bow. The following extract describes very clearly that the Indians in New England employed the primary release. "For their shooting they be most desperate marksmen for a point blancke object, and if it may bee possible *Cornicum oculos configere* they will doe it: such is their celerity and dexterity in Artillerie, that they can smite the swift running Hinde and nimble winked Pigeon without a standing pause or left eyed blinking; they draw their Arrowes between the fore fingers and the thumbe; their bowes be quicke, but not very strong, not killing above six or seven score". (p. 97)

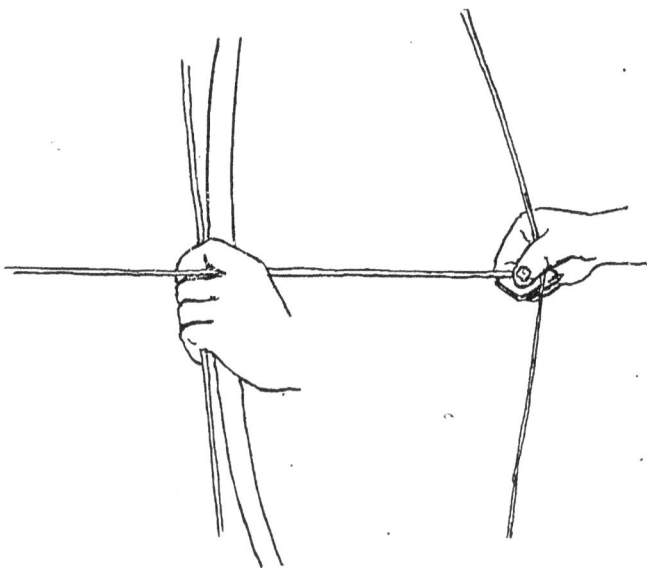

Fig. 6 Micmac

I am indebted to DR. S. J. MIXTER for a photograph of a Micmac Indian who illustrated to him the method of drawing the arrow. It shows the typical primary release. (Fig. 6.) The Indian was one of the oldest Micmacs in the Cascapedia settlement in Canada. He told DR. MIXTER that other tribes in Canada used the same method and he knew of no other. These facts I mentioned in my first paper but the figure which was not published at that time is now given.

In a supplement to the *International Archieves of Ethnology*, Vol. XVII, is a memoir by DR. C. H. DEGOEJE, on the "Ethnology of The Surinam Indians." A large number of arrows are figured and these have a raised ring of fibre at their nock ends indicating the primary release.

Fig. 7   Tierra del Fuego

The Ona tribe of Tierra del Fuego practiced the primary release and also the tertiary release as show in the illustrations of these savages in a book entitled, "Through the First Antarctic Night", by FREDERICK A. COOK, M. D.   Figure 7 is a rough copy of one of the illustrations in the book.

In the British Museum is an arrow from Tierra Del Fuego, collected by Mr. H. N. Moseley in 1876. This arrow is 27¼ inches long. It has two short and wide barbs parallel to the nock. A shoulder of fibre and gum near the nock would indicate the primary release. (Fig. 8.)

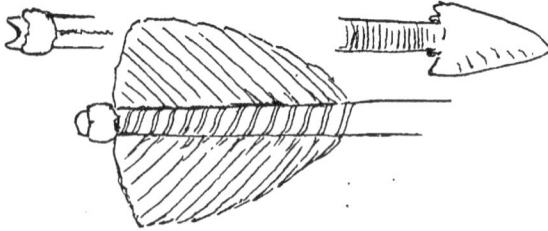

Fig. 8   Tierra del Fuego

From photographs shown me at the Hamburg Museum of natives of the Solomon Islands in the act of shooting the method of release was primary.

At the Paris Exposition of 1889 were many negroes from the French Protectorates, Africa. Among these were negroes from Senegal and from them I got their method of release which was primary, the bow was held nearly horizontal.

In Sir Samuel Baker's book, "Albert Nyanza," Page 63, is the following description of the archery of the Africans of that region. "Fortunately the natives are bad archers......the string is never drawn with the two forefingers as in most countries, but is simply pulled by holding the arrow between the middle joint of the forefinger and thumb." This clear description indicates the primary release.

I am greatly indebted to Mr. Kimpei Otsu, Chief of the Aboriginal Bureau of Formosa and to Mr. S. Ishii, of Kaihoku, of Formosa, for a number of interesting photographs representing the savages of that Island in the act of drawing the bow. Seven of these photographs represent members of the Vonum tribe of various villages.

10

These are indicated as domesticated savages, all of these but one are using the primary release. (Fig. 9.) The one exception is drawing the arrow with the left hand and all four fingers are bent over the string suggesting a modification of the tertiary release. Two others are marked head-hunters belonging to the Taiyal, or tattooed tribe. These are also practicing the primary release.

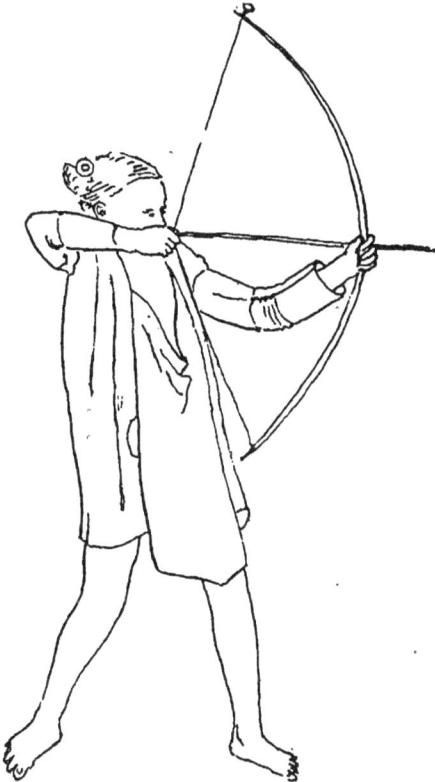

Fig. 9 Formosa

In the Trocadero Museum, in Paris, is a curious arrow from Formosa made by the savage Botans. The nock end is cut in long

11

shallow gashes giving a firmer grip of the thumb and forefinger. This form indicates the use of the primary release. (Fig. 10.)

In using the primary release, as I have already shown, the arrow is usually knobbed or the nock end of the arrow where the thumb and finger grasp it is roughened by slight cuts, or gashes to ensure a stronger hold on the arrow.

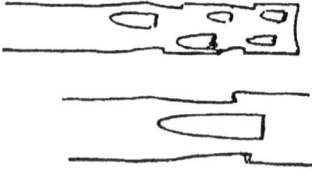

Fig. 10   Formosa

In studying the remarkable collection of Danish antiquities in the Museum of Northern Antiquities, at Copenhagen, we found an exhaustive collection of objects from the peat bogs of Denmark. So abundant are these remains that STEENSTRUP estimated that every column of peat, three feet square at the surface, would yield some evidence of human workmanship. In the collection were a number of long bows, round in section, with a slight notch at either end. These bows with their arrows were mounted on tablets and were believed to be about 2000 years old. The arrows were of special interest, they were rather thick and clumsily made but the constriction of

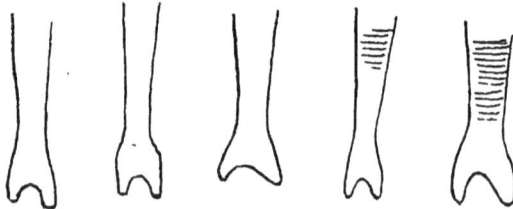

Fig. 11   Peat bogs, Denmark

the shaft before reaching the nock end was very noticeable. Of great interest to me was the fact that every arrow was distinctly knobbed and enlarged at the nock end, (Fig. 11) showing that these ancient people had not acquired the Mediterranean release which would have been difficult with this form of arrow. They were using the primary release of their savage ancestors. MR. VILHELM BOYE,

12

an officer of the Museum, told me that the arrows had only two barbs. No trace of the barbs were seen, though a close examination with the poor light at the time showed that the nock end of the arrow had been wound with a fibre of some kind.

At the Kiel Museum there was a fine collection of peat bog relics from Schleswig. Here also I was permitted to make sketches of arrows, all of which showed the same enlargement of the nock end, though quite different in shape from the Danish forms, indicating the same method of release, namely, the primary. (Fig 12.) Their age dated from 217 A. D., as determined by coins associated with them.

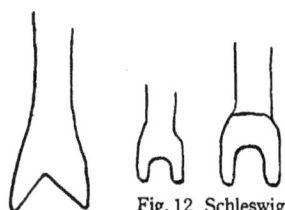

Fig. 12 Schleswig

In Figure 13, I give rough tracings of the nock ends of the arrows of various tribes of North American Indians, all showing enlargement of the nock ends of the arrows, indicating the use of the primary release. In some cases the knobbed arrow might indicate the use of the secondary release but in that release with the use of two extra

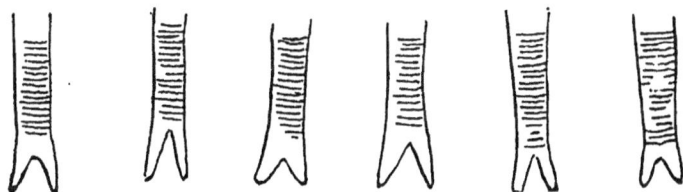

Fig. 13 North American Indians

fingers in pulling the bow the enlargement of the arrow was not so necessary.

Figure 14 illustrates in a marked degree the use of the primary release. It represents an arrow used by the Thlingit tribe of Alaska. It was collected by LIEUT. G. T. EMMONS, U. S. A. and is in the collection of the U. S. National Museum. It is interesting as showing that these people in close proximity to the Eskimo who used the Medi-

13

terranean release had never acquired the more powerful form but retained the primary form. A parallel case is shown by the Ainu method of drawing the bow. Though associated with the Japanese for nearly 2000 years they had never acquired the more effective Mongolian release but adhered to the primary form.

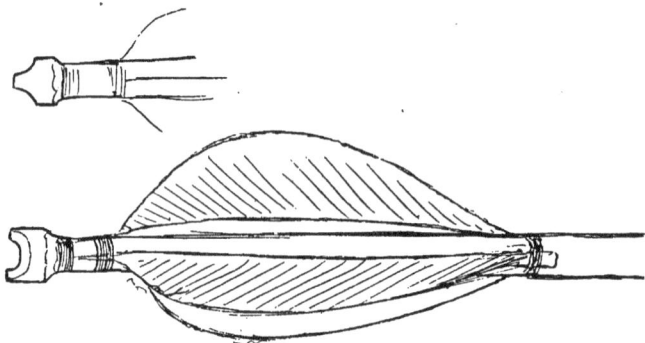

Fig. 14 Aiaska

PROF. E. N. HORSFORD informed me that when he was a boy his father was a missionary among the Seneca Indians in New York. He often played and shot with the Indian boys, the target generally consisting of a big copper cent held in a cleft stick. The practice of drawing the bow was with the thumb and bent forefinger pinching the arrow and two other fingers assisting in drawing the string, a distinct secondary release.

LIEUT. SCHAWATKA, an arctic explorer, who had traveled in Mexico told me that the Baramos Indians, a tribe of the Tarahumari, living in southwestern Chihuahua practiced the secondary release.

The Menomini Indians who now live on their reservation in north central Wisconsin have been minutely studied by MR. ALANSON SKINNER and the results form a monograph in the publications of the Museum of the American Indian, Heye Foundation. The Indians are typical Algonquin people and MR. SKINNER states that they use the tertiary release while the neighboring Ojibwa use the primary and secondary releases.

14

In an interesting article by CARL LUMHOLTZ, in *Scribner's Magazine*, Vol. XIV, 1894, entitled "Tarahumari Dances and Plant Worship," he gives a picture of an Indian using the bow. The method of release is clearly depicted and represents the tertiary release. Tracings of figures in certain ancient Mexican codices sent me by MRS. ZELIA NUTTALL represent the tertiary release.

PROF. W. JOEST, of Berlin, kindly sent me some observations he made regarding the arrow release of indians and bush negroes of Surinam. In his letter he makes the distinction between the Arawaks, Caribs, and Galibes of the coast and interior of Surinam and of the Upper Maroni which he calls indians, and the inhabitants of Surinam and the Upper Maroni which he designates as bush negroes. They no longer use arrows and bows as weapons, but only for shooting fish, small deer, turtle, tapir, birds, etc. He says: "I observed a remarkable difference between Indians and 'Bosch.' The American aborigine, Arawaks, as well as Caribs, keep the bow horizontally, the 'Bosch,' whose ancestors were imported from Africa, vertically. Both put the arrow at the upper or left side of the bow; both keep the arrow steady with the forefinger of the left hand, the palm of course undermost. The way of pulling corresponds to your 'tertiary release' with the difference that Indians and Bush negroes use all their four fingers while the thumb (stretched) helps the forefinger. The forefinger is nearly straight. I had the impression that the forefinger and thumb were only keeping the arrow in its position whilst the 3rd, 4th and 5th fingers were really pulling." He found an astonishing number of the Bush negroes were left-handed. They accordingly put the arrow at the right side of the bow. He thinks no difference exists between the natives of Guyara in the method of release.

DR. THOMAS BARBOUR, in his travels in New Guinea, secured a photograph of a Papuan in the act of shooting the bow. The release is with the thumb pressed against the arrow and all four fingers bearing on the string, the arrow being between the thumb and forefinger. This represents the tertiary release. This release varies as does the Mediterranean form. In both releases two, three and even four fingers may be used in drawing the string, though rarely is the little finger used. (Fig. 15).

FELIX SPEISER in his "Two Years with the Natives in the Western Pacific" represents the arrow release of the natives of Santa Cruz, an island between the Solomon Islands and the New Hebrides. Figures of two men are given in the act of drawing the bow, the attitude of the fingers on the string is given in the clearest manner and represents the tertiary release. The middle finger is slightly overlapping the forefinger.

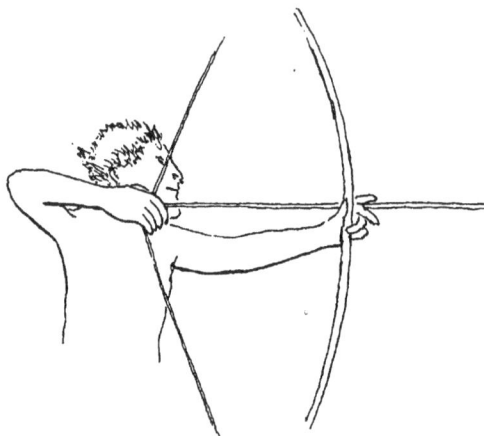

Fig. 15   Papuan

From a photograph in the Ethnological Museum at Berlin I copied the arrow release of the Kaders of India. The Kaders are a primitive tribe living among the Ammali Hills, north of Tiruwanduram on the western side of India. It resembles somewhat the release of the Bakuba and Basonge people of Africa brought back by LIEUT. WISSMANN. The four fingers are over the string, the forefinger slightly flexed and pressing the arrow against the bow, the thumb inactive. It must be classed with the tertiary release. (Fig. 16.) The Kaders used a heavy bow, the arrows are iron-pointed and four-barbed.

PROF. F. W. WILLIAMS, of Yale, when he was in Rangoon, Burma, sent me a postal card on which was depicted an archer shooting a bow, the forefinger was extended along the arrow while the other three fingers were flexed over the string. It may be regarded as a slight modification of the tertiary release. MR. WILLIAMS writes: "Here is an arrow release that appears to be the real thing, but I have yet to see one of the natives shoot. The picture is lettered "A Burmese Villager."

DR. KARL VON DEN STEINEN, in his work on "The Savages of Central Brazil" says; (p. 230) "The bow is generally held downward. The arrow lies to the left of the bow. It is held by the second and third fingers, while the fourth and fifth fingers help to steady the cord for the aim, the thumb is not used at all. This

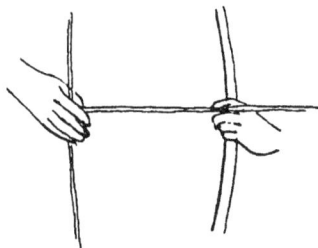

Fig. 16 Kader, India

way of holding the bow and arrow which is used in the Middle Sea, of which E. S. MORSE speaks is different from that of the Bororo. Any contrivance to keep the fingers from being rubbed by the cord is not used. The left hand which holds the bow can hold a number of arrows in reserve." The release is typically tertiary. (Fig. 17). I had the pleasure of meeting MR. STEINEN and he told me that he explored a new region in Brazil which had never reached the Age of Iron.

At the Ethnological Museum, in Amsterdam, I learned that the Javanese practice the tertiary release using the index finger only, a weak method and implying the use of the lightest of bows. The nock of the arrow is very deep and narrow indicating a light string. The bow had a heavy thickening in the middle, deeply grooved for four fingers, and was covered with black velvet; an effeminate bow and probably used by women. In the Copenhagen Museum I saw an arrow from Java with nock shallow and flaring.

In 1889 I met at the Ethnological Museum in Berlin, LIEUT. WISSMANN and DR. LUDWIG WOLF, recently returned from the interior of Africa with valuable collections of ethnological material and they assured me that the Bakuba people and the Basonge people, in Central Africa used a release, which represented a slight modification of the tertiary release. The bow is held vertical, the forefinger presses

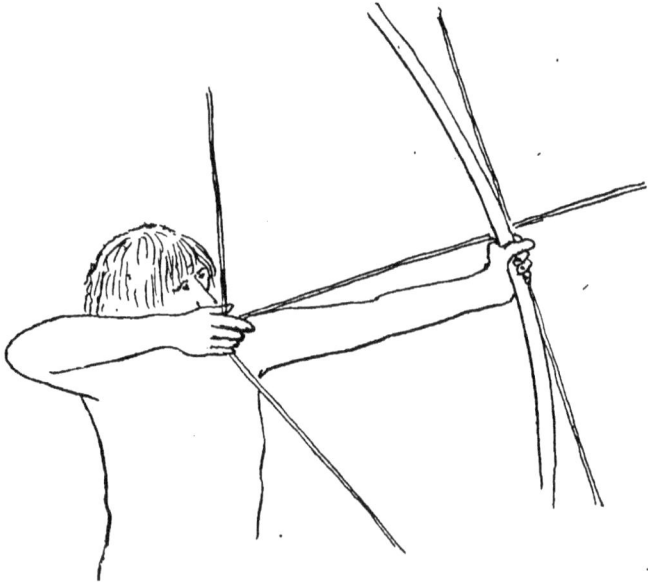

Fig. 17 Bororo, Brazil

the arrow against the bow, the arrow being on the right side of the bow. The bow is strong and the arrow beautifully made having three barbs. LIEUT. WISSMANN told me that in shooting, the archer first points the arrow to the ground in drawing, and then quickly raises and discharges it. The Baluba tribe in Africa uses the Mediterranean release, two-fingered. The bow resembles that of the ancient Egyptian.

It would be an interesting path of inquiry to trace the origin of the Mediterranean release. Did it first arise among the Aryan people in Central Asia and if so was the release transmitted to the Eskimo? It is a curious fact that the Eskimo savages ranging from the east to the west coasts of North America practice the Mediterranean release to the exclusion of all other forms. The Mediterranean release occurs sporadically the world over. Furthermore the Eskimo are the only people who have ever devised a special form of arrow, flattened at the nock end to more easily facilitate the discharge of the arrow, it would be almost impossible to use this form of arrow in other releases. We have seen that in prehistoric times the Danes and the inhabitants of Schleswig practiced the primary release and probably the method of other European races. Mr. John Murdock, who made an ethnological journey to Point Barrow in Alaska, and lived with the Eskimo for two years believed in Scandinavian influences among the Eskimo. In a letter to me he says, "You are quite at liberty to allude to my ideas of Scandinavian influence among the Eskimo. I have not studied up the the Scandinavian side of the question thoroughly enough to make any formal statement on the subject." Mr. Murdock gave particular attention to Eskimo arts and customs in a report published by the Smithsonian Institution. In this report he is strongly inclined to the belief that several customs extending from Greenland to and across Bering Straits are derived from Scandinavian colonists in Greenland. These are "the method of arrow release, the size of the oars as well as paddles, a custom as far as I know, unparalleled among savages, and the method of slinging the oar in thongs instead of using rowlocks. The sail of the Umiak is also strikingly like those in the Norse ships."

We have seen that the early Scandinavian release was primary, is it unreasonable to suggest that the Mediterranean release may have been first practiced by the Eskimo and from this race the races to the south acquired it? If in paleochrystic ice or prehistoric Eskimo deposits we could find the flattened nock end of an arrow it might settle the question.

Fig. 18　Seri　Gulf of California

It is a curious fact that the release universally practiced by the Mediterranean nations, and a release which I thought was associated with the higher races is also seen among the lowest savage races today, namely, the Andaman Islanders, the Pygmy negritos of the Philippine Islands, the Veddahs of Ceylon, the Botocudo Indians of Brazil and other low savage peoples.

Fig. 19   Apache

On an island in the Gulf of California is found the remnant of a tribe known as the Seri Indians. A voluminous report of these Indians was published in the *17th Annual Report of the U. S. Bureau of Ethnology*, by DR. WM. MCGEE. MAJOR POWELL, as Chief of the Bureau, in an introductory note to the *Report* says, "Among these aborigines known to Caucasians the Seri Indians appear to stand nearly or quite at the bottom of the scale. They are without agricultural or other organized industries: they still haunt their primeval shorelands, and their fisheries are crude and simple, while their water-craft (in which their culture culminates) are practically individual in design, manufacture and function; and their social organization is of peculiarly significant simplicity." In this report one figure is given of a Seri warrior in the attitude of shooting the bow. A perfect Mediterranean release is shown. (Fig. 18).

DR. TEN KATE sent me a photograph of an Apache warrior from San Carlos, Arizona. He is in the act of shooting the bow. (Fig. 19). The release is clearly Mediterranean using three fingers.

DR. BOVALLIUS, of Stockholm, described to me a release which may have been identical to that described by DR. STEINEN, namely,

21

a two-fingered Mediterranean. This was practiced by a tribe of Indians on the south-eastern coast of Costa Rica known as the Talamanca Indians, Bribri tribe. He was sure of the release as he had often shot with them. They·use this release in shooting fish in the water. The arrow is six feet long and without barbs, and is held between the tips of the first and second fingers, the thumb is held at the butt of the arrow which is truncate. The end of the arrow is slightly thickened with gum and cord so as to give a firmer hold. The bow is held nearly horizontal. (Fig. 20). Despite the statement of DR. BOVALLIUS as to

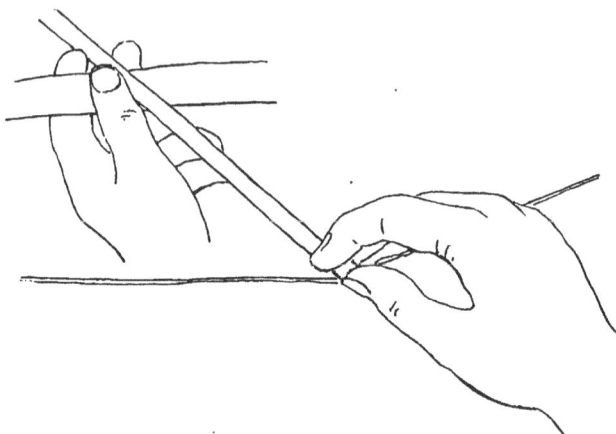

Fig. 20   Bribri

the method of release of the Talamanca Indians we find in the *National Geographic Magazine*, Vol. XLI, No. 2, an article by PAUL B. POPENOE, on Costa Rica in which is given a picture of these Indians. In some respects the picture agrees with DR. BOVALLIUS' statements; the arrows are six feet long, they are evidently shooting fish but the attitude of the hand in all three indicates the tertiary release.

At Manchester, England, I met a traveler, whose name I have misplaced, who told me he had been among the Botocudo Indians of Brazil, and he had observed that in using the bow they drew it with two fingers on the cord, which indicated the Mediterranean release.

22

WILLIAM JNO. STEAINS, employed by an English firm in constructing a railway in Brazil undertook, at his own expense, the exploration of the Rio Doce and its tributaries. This valley is inhabited by wild Botucudo Indians. These Indians practice the Mediterranean release using two fingers unless the bow is very stiff when three fingers are used.

In STRUTTS "Sports and Pastimes" there is the figure of an archer copied from Saxon Manuscript of the eighth century. The release shows three fingers on the string with the arrow between the first and second fingers, indicating a typical Mediterranean release. Usually the figures of ancient archers show only two fingers.

MRS. CLEMENT WATERS sent me a photograph of the bronze doors of the famous cathedral at Amalfi. These doors were made in Constantinople in 1075 A. D. Among the paneled figures is an archer plainly showing the Mediterranean release and probably showing the use of the two fingers. The figures are very archaic. The designs were evidently made by one who was not a Turk as the Turks practice the Mongolian release.

In a famous psalter executed by GEOFFREY LONTERELL, in 1345, the figure of an archer is given shooting at a target, the Mediterranean release is clearly shown. Three fingers are used instead of two as in most of the figures over two hundred years old.

In the Royal Art Museum, Berlin, are a number of ancient Greek vases, red on black, on which an archer is shown using the typical Mediterranean release. In the same Museum is a bronze statue of Eros bracing the bow in English style. The bow being short the lower end rests against the knee instead of the foot.

In the Museum of St. Germain, near Paris, is a remarkable replica of Trajan's Column, in this the Dacians are shown using the Mediterranean release, two fingered. In many of the figures represented the bow is very short.

Realizing that the aboriginal tribes of India were Aryan in origin it was most important to ascertain the methods of archery among the savage tribes in the interior. An East Indian officer, CAPT.

23

JOHN JOHNSTONE, visiting Boston, promised to secure for me, through a brother officer, the method of arrow release of primitive tribes inhabiting the region in which he was stationed. Some months after CAPT. JOHNSTONE'S departure I got a letter from him, accompanied by the clearest drawings showing the arrow release among the native tribes. The following is an extract, "I asked a friend of mine, CAPT. LUARD, who is compiling the Gazeteer of Central India to have some sketches prepared for me for transmission to you and he has sent those I enclose, together with two photographs. I hope they will be of some use to you. The Bhils (pronounced Bheels) are among the most primitive tribes of Central India and are looked upon as aborigines. They do not admit themselves to be Hindus, though when brought into close contact with the latter they are apt to adopt many Hindu customs and deities. They still use bows and arrows in their native haunts chiefly against wild beasts, but occasionally against each other." The following figure (Fig. 21) is a reduced reproduction of one of the drawings. The release is an absolutely perfect Mediterranean with two fingers.

In a collection of photographs published by the London Indian Museum in 1868, entitled "The People of India." Vol. 1, Plate 21, is shown a native of the Korwa group from Chola Nagpoor and regarded as an aborigine; the release is typically Mediterranean.

EDWARD TUITE DALTON, in a work entitled "Descriptive Ethnology of Bengal," figures a number of the Korwas shooting with a bow. These people are considered one of the wildest of the Kolarian tribes. The arrow release is clearly shown and it is distinctly Mediterranean. The Korwas are found in the hills rising in the Sirguja and Jaspur Estates in the Province of Shutia, Nagpur.

EDWARD HORACE MANN, Esq., in his work "On the Aboriginal Inhabitants of the Andaman Islands"* says, "It is a singular fact that the mode in which the tribes of Great Andaman discharge their arrows differs from that in vogue among the Jar'awa. While the latter are

*Reprinted from the *Journal of the Anthropological Institute of Great Britain and Ireland.*

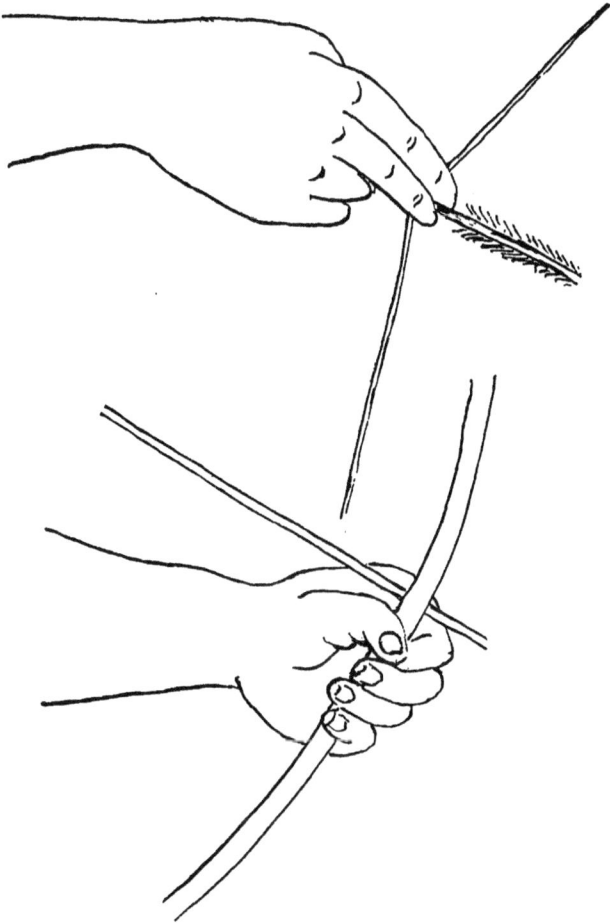

Fig. 21   Bhil, India

said to adopt the plan usual among ourselves of holding the nock of the arrow inside the string by means of the middle joints of the fore and middle fingers and drawing the string with the same joints, it is the practice among the former to place the arrows in position between the thumb and the top joint of the forefinger and to draw the string to the mouth with the middle and third fingers." The Jar'awa then practice the Mediterranean release while the others practice the secondary release. As an illustration of the instability of arrow release among

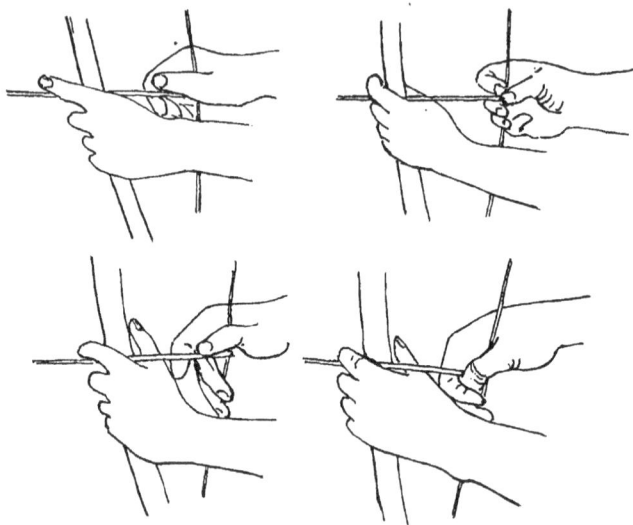

Fig. 22 Andaman

savages, I refer to the archery number of the Badminton series in which MR. LONGMAN presents some reproductions of photographs taken by MR. M. V. PORTMAN from his unpublished notes. These I have copied, (Fig. 22) and they represent in turn the primary, a modification of the tertiary, Mediterranean and Mongolian, and the one described above is certainly secondary. It may be of interest to remark that here is one of the lowest savage groups of people, the only pure negrito people existing, so MR. PORTMAN says, so low that they are in

26

an amorphous condition regarding archery. A crooked wooden stave for a bow, arrows without barbs and, according to MR. PORTMAN, who lived among them for fourteen years, the poorest shots imaginable

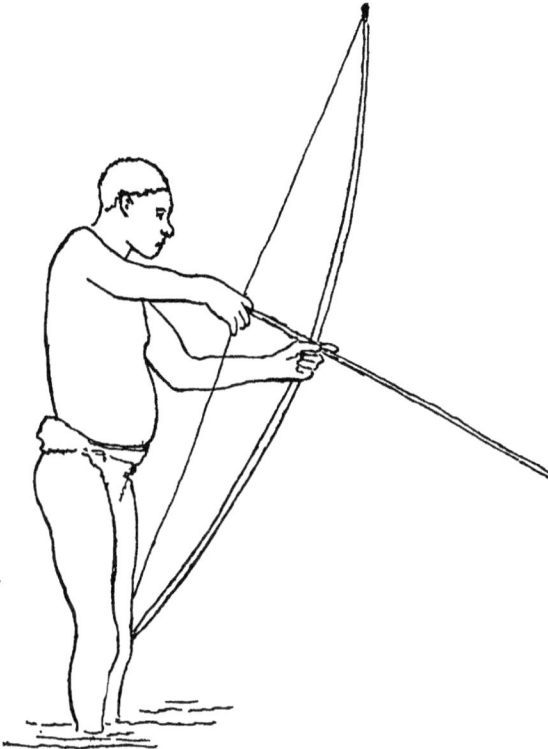

Fig. 23   Inge, Little Andaman

and yet presenting examples of the five pronounced releases known. They are in such an embryonic condition that they have not yet established a permanent release. The Onge Tribe inhabiting the Little Andaman practice the Mediterranean release (Fig. 23).

In the third volume of *Ratzel's History of Mankind*, page 356, is an illustration of a Veddah of Ceylon in the act of shooting the bow.

The photograph from which it was derived was made by EMIL SCHMIDT of Leipsic. The release is Mediterranean, three fingered. (Fig. 24).

At the St. Louis Fair I saw members of a tribe called Bagoba from the Philippines. One of them shot for me and he used the primary

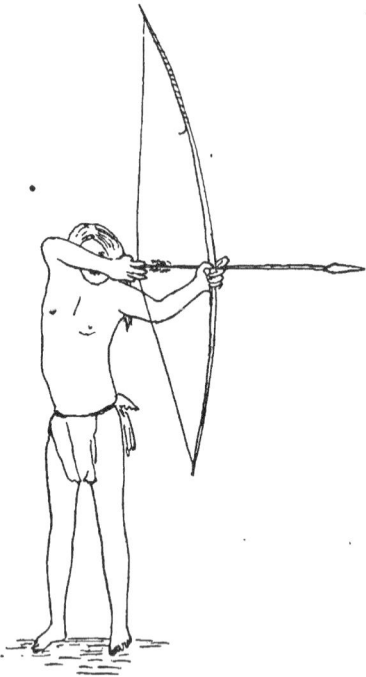

Fig. 24   Veddah   F g. 25   Negrito

release. The arrows were not feathered and their flight was crooked. A negrito child among them, 19 months old, shot for me in the most vigorous manner. He used the tertiary release with thumb on the string, the bow held vertical. (Fig. 25).

28

MR. VERNER, at the St. Louis Fair had charge of a number of pygmies from the Philippines. A number of the tribe known as Chiri shot for me using the Mediterranean release. (Fig. 26. See frontispiece.) The best shots among them used the tertiary release.

In the Ethnological Museum at Dresden I copied from a photograph an Aeta (Negrito) from Cagayan, Northern Luzon, in the act of shooting and he used a typical Mediterranean release. (Fig 27).

In the *Smithsonian Annual Report* for 1899 (p. 540) is a picture of a Negrito from the Province of Maravale, Luzon. The release shown is Mediterranean.

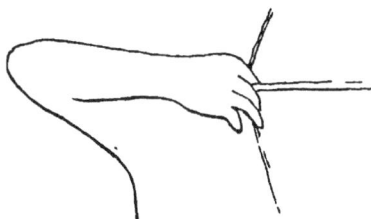

Fig. 27   Negrito

In *Collier's Weekly*, for May 13, 1899 is a picture of a Tinguian bowman of the Philippine Islands. The release shown is distinctly Mediterranean, two fingered.

In photographs of the marvellous ruins at Angkor, Cambogia, I found the figure of an archer drawing the bow and the release is plainly Mediterranean. These ruins date back to the ninth century. One might have looked for a Mongolian release. When I first defined the Mongolian release I supposed it was strictly limited to Asiatic nations. DR. FELIX VON LUSCHAN, Director of the Ethnological Museum of Berlin, in a letter to me dated July 16, 1891 announced the discovery of the Mongolian release in Africa. The following is an extract from his letter, "I am sending you a paper model of a quite new form of arrow release. It came to the Museum some days ago. I will have it photographed and published in the Transactions of our

Anthropological Society, but it will be several months before it comes out, and I want you to know it as soon as possible. Our specimens came from the Wootah people (interior of Kameroun, West Africa) and were brought here by LIEUT. MORGEN. You might best call them rings for the metacarpus although they are not round. They consist of a small thin board of hard wood from four to five millimeters in thickness. This board is bent near its middle so as to form a yoke, both sides remaining quite parallel and being held together by a thin leather string, which may be tightened or loosened according to the size of the hand which is to enter. The hand enters with all four fingers, the forefinger on the side of the round angle, the little finger on the open side, naturally the broad end which is generally ornamented and comes on the dorsum manus. I hope the description is plain enough so that you may understand this marvellous kind of release. It is by far the most powerful I ever heard of, because you engage the whole hand and not only one or two fingers, and still the instant of loosing the arrow is exceedingly delicate and smooth. I think that when one has once seen this release one will find it preferable to all others, according to the form of their bows and the immense force they can employ. The Wootah have also quite enormous leather bracelets for the protection of the bow hand. A section of such a bracelet would have the form you see here (Fig. 28) only the small ovoid part forms the real bracelet, the rest is a hollow cone of thick black leather which is also ornamented with much care and taste." The *Transactions of the Berlin Society of Anthropology* published his paper on the "Bending of the Bow," a free translation of a portion of which is given in the end of this paper in an appendix.

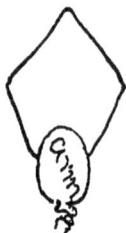

Fig. 28

I have already called attention to the fact that in indistinct rock sculpture or drawings the attitude of the hand resembles more or less a closed fist, while in the Mongolian release the fingers appear to be bent downward, the back of the hand being uppermost. In a stone sculpture of a Hittite archer discovered by DR. LUSCHAN, and with

30

his permission figured by MR. LONGMAN in "Badminton's Archery,"
p. 67, the attitude of the hand indicates the Mongolian release. This
figure was discovered in Asia Minor. The expression on the face of this
Hittite figure recalls ROGER ASCHAM'S description in his Toxophilus,
written in 1544, of his squad of awkward bowmen. Among other
grotesque expressions, he says, "Some make a face with wrything theyr
mouth as though they were doing you wotte what." (Fig. 29).

MR. RUDOLPH VIRCHOW permitted me to make a drawing of a

Fig. 29   Hittite Archer

bronze ax in his possession which was dug up in the Caucasus. It was
believed to date a thousand years, B.C., the age being determined by
coins associated with it. Upon its face was an incised outline of an
archer of which I made a rubbing. Both hands were upon the string
but the outline was so faint and so roughly drawn that it was impossible to determine the method of release; the bow was very short but
certainly not Mongolian. The peculiar head-dress or helmet may be
identified by some classical archaeologist.

31

MR. F. W. GOOKIN, of Chicago, has kindly sent me a copy of a Persian archer from ALFRED MASKELL'S "Hand book of Russian Art and Art Objects in Russia." The archer is delicately engraved on an ancient silver bowl of Sassanian workmanship in the Hermitage Museum, Petrograd. MR. GOOKIN, in a letter, says "The description of the bowl which is very meagre states that it bears an inscription in Pehlir characters (the ancient writing used in Persia under the dynasty of the Sassanians) which has not been deciphered, the date therefore is uncertain, but from a comparison with a monument known under the name of Takt-i Bostan situated near the modern town of Kermanschat, which was executed during the reign of BAHRAN KERMANSCHAT

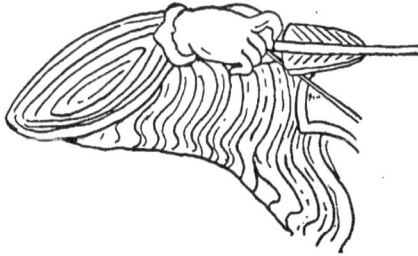

Fig. 30   Sassanian

(A. D. 389-399) it is supposed to have been made about the same period." MR. GOOKIN'S exquisite drawing is difficult to reproduce on account of the delicacy of the lines. He has made an enlarged copy of the right hand showing clearly the Mongolian release (Fig. 30). The thumb is seen curving up and the forefinger is locked over the end of the thumb. The bow is strictly Mongolian in character and hence a composite bow. This evidence of the Mongolian release establishes a date showing at least how early the method was introduced from China, for unquestionably being Aryan, in still earlier times the Mediterranean, and before this the primary release must have been used.

The most complete and satisfactory description of an arrow release, and all details of an archer's practice is given by SAXTON T. POPE in the *University of California Publications in American*

Anthropology and Ethnology, Vol. 13, No. 3. In this Memoir, entitled "Yahi Archery," MR. POPE gives the results of a study of the last survivor of a tribe of Indians with whom MR. POPE associated for three years. The author says, "The present paper is an attempt to present the facts concerning the archery of one tribe, the Yahi or Deer Creek Indians of north central California, the most southerly division of the Yanan stock as represented in the person of its last survivor, ISHI, who lived from 1911 to 1916 at the University of California."

MR. POPE lived with ISHI for three years, hunted with him in the woods and watched him as he fabricated his bows and arrows, illustrating all the details in his paper. A colored plate is given of 18 arrowheads made from flint and obsidian. The incredible precision and delicacy in the making of these arrowheads almost exceeds belief. MR. POPE'S "Memoir" is really a monograph of the archery of a single tribe. In shooting, the bow was held in a horizontal position with the back of the hand downward, the arrow resting on the bow between the thumb and forefinger. MR. POPE says, "The arrow release was a modification of that known as the Mongolian type, that is he 'drew' the bow with the right thumb flexed beneath the string. On the thumb nail he laid the end of the middle finger, to strengthen the hold. The index finger, completely flexed, rested on the arrow to keep it from slipping from the string. The extremities of the feathers, being near the nock, were neatly folded along the shaft in the grip of these fingers, to prevent them from being ruffled." The outline, (Fig. 31), traced from his drawing clearly illustrates the position of the fingers. I do not regard this release as a modification of the Mongolian release but a new and distinct form, its only resemblance is seen in drawing the string with the thumb, the thumb-ring, which is invariably used in the Mongolian release, is absent. It is a distinct type and as MR. POPE is the discoverer of it I leave it to him to name this new species. MR. POPE says that "ISHI knew of several releases, saying that certain other tribes used them. The primary type, that where the arrow butt is gripped between the thumb and the flexed forefinger, he said certain Indians used, and it seemed to be a criterion of strength." The most extraordinary feature of ISHI's use of the bow is that on the discharge of the arrow the bow is made to revolve in the hand as in the Japanese practice. He says, "When the arrow left the string, at the moment of release, the bow revolved, or turned over completely, in his hand, so that the back of the bow was toward him." The Japanese are the only people who cause the bow to revolve in the hand except those who use the stone bow. In this release no arm guard is required and MR. POPE said ISHI "never used a wrist guard or, bracer, on his left arm to protect it from the string, although he nearly always pulled up his shirt sleeve.

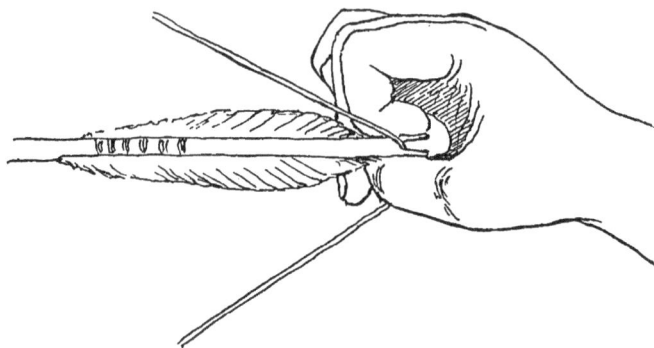

Fig. 31 Yahi California

This was to avoid striking any clothing with the string, which would check the flight of the arrow. At times the string did strike his forearm, and bruise it, and after prolonged shooting his left wrist was often sore and ecchymosed."

It is a curious linguistic coincidence that the name ISHI is identical to a Japanese word, meaning stone, and the first syllable of his tribal name, Yahi, Ya, is the Japanese word for arrow.

In gathering material for a chapter on archers' thumb-rings I made hasty sketches of these objects in European museums as opportunity offered. On writing up these notes I was amazed at the scant literature on the subject.* With the exception of DR. FELIX VON LUSCHAN'S paper on African thumb-rings in which he illustrates two from Africa and a new type from Korea, I found only a few archers' rings figured. In MEYRICK'S "Ancient Armour," 1842, is figured a ring accredited to Persia. HANSARD'S "Archery," 1845, copies it and in my "Ancient and Modern Methods of Arrow Release," 1885, I reproduced it from MEYRICK'S work. I may add that the figure bears but little resemblance to the archer's thumb-ring, doubtless owing to poor drawing. In a work entitled "Projectile-Throwing Engines of the Ancients," with a treatise on the Turkish and other oriental bows, by

*"The *sefin*, or thumb-rings, before alluded to, are one of the distinctions of an Oriental archer. Englishmen, it is well known, draw the bowstring with their first three fingers; the Flemings, with the first and second only; but neither use the thumb at all. The Asiatic method is the reverse of this. There the bowman draws altogether with his thumb, the forefinger bent in its first and second joint, being merely pressed on one side of the arrow nock, to secure it from falling. In order to prevent the flesh from being torn by the bowstring, he wears a broad ring of agate, cornelian, green marble, ivory, horn, or iron, according to his rank and means. Upon the inside of this, which projects half an inch, the string rests when the bow is drawn; on the outside it is only half that breadth; and, in loosing the arrow, he straightens his thumb, which sets the string free. These rings, with a spare string, are usually carried in a small box, suspended at the bowman's side; but from habit, many retain them constantly upon the hand, for ornament as well as use.

Consistent with the splendour of their other appointments, the sefin worn by those dark-eyed houris, whose feats we have so recently been contemplating, are adorned with all the cunning of the jeweller's art. A stone called jadde, crystal, jasper, and even gold, inlaid with stones of varied hue, glitter in the sunbeams as each snowy hand strains up the silken bowstring. A quilted half sleeve of crimson velvet, or fine cloth, thickly embroidered with gold flowers, protects the arm from being bruised by the cord in its return. Did not a very curious relic, recently come to light, prove CHAUCER's 'gai bracer' to be a purely English fashion, we might imagine he was describing one of these. The weight of the gold in one which I wore upon my arm for a short time was remarkable; it probably amounted to three or four ounces." Hansard Book of Archery, p. 136.

In no other country in the world has the practice of archery survived as in England. The Royal Toxophilite Society of London and many other archery Societies in England were founded in the 17th and 18th centuries. England may claim the greatest number of books on archery. With this supremacy in the archery field it is strange to find so brief an article on the subject in the Encyclopedia Brittanica. The word archer's ring does not appear. Its meagre bibliography makes no mention of HANSARD'S classical book with its steel engravings. In some unaccountable way it records my "Ancient and Modern Methods of Arrow Release" *Essex Institute Bulletin*, Salem, Mass., 1885, as follows: Archery, Ancient and Modern, E. S. Morse, Worcester, Mass. 1792.

SIR RALPH PAINE-GALLWAY, 1907, an archer's ring is figured on a hand supposed to represent its attitude. The ring is on the thumb upside down and the attitude of the hand is entirely wrong. Most detailed and elaborate descriptions and illustrations are, however, given of the catapult, balista, trebuchet and other ancient engines of war.

DR. BERTHOLD LAUFER, in his memoir on Jade (Field Museum of Natural History, Anthropological Series, Vol. X.) figures an archer's thumb-ring from a tomb of the Han period. It is flattened on one side, the flattened surface being slightly rounded. MR. LAUFER in quoting from a Chinese book by WU TA-CHENG, says: "These thumb-rings are still used in archery and manufactured in Peking from the antlers of an elk." "WU TA-CHENG figures also a specimen of pure white jade..... and arrived at the conclusion that this particular piece was reserved for Imperial use, on the ground that such rings of white jade were permitted to the Emperor only, while those of the officials were of ivory." "The mode of wearing the ring may be seen in a Chinese illustration given by P. ETIENNE ZI (*Pratique des examens militaires en Chine, Shanghai* 1896). Father ZI remarks that the most prized rings are those made of jade of the Han period, of a white gray with red veins and green stripes; those taken from the graves of students who have graduated at the time of the military examinations are reddish in color, and a notion that they afford protection against spirits is attached to them."

In the Pitt-River's collection, University Museum, Oxford, DR. HENRY BALFOUR called my attention to a white jade ring accredited to India which is the only one I have ever seen of its kind. Its peculiarity consists in having a deep groove on the face of the ring to engage the bow string. A blunt projecting ridge is seen on the back of the ring. It is probably Persian in origin. Fig. 32. It is somewhat flat in form like a number of the Persian rings figured in the following plates.

In volume second of the two huge volumes forming the Catalogue of the Bishop Collection of jade a figure is given of an archer's ring, brownish in color, with the statement that it was found in an ancient tomb of the Han period.

In BADMINTON'S "Archery," COL. H. WALDRON, contributes an exhaustive bibliography of works on archery including treatises, not only books but society reports, magazines and even newspaper articles. On an examination of this voluminous list I failed to find any reference to an archer's ring.

LORD EDGARTON published "A Description of India and Oriental Armour", in 1896. The volume is illustrated with beautiful colored

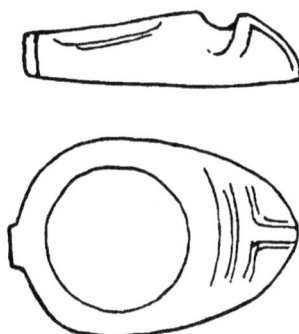

Fig. 32   Thumb ring India (?)

plates besides many in black.   Over one thousand catalogue numbers are given, comprising those of the Indian Museum of London, and those of his own collection, yet no reference to an archer's ring is mentioned. This seems the more strange as I sketched two thumb-rings in the Indian Museum.   It is true that the collection of the Indian Museum has been transferred to the South Kensington Museum, but one should have found the rings mentioned in the numbered catalogue in LORD EDGARTON'S book.

I have sketches of archers' rings from the British Museum accredited to India.   Some of them are beautifully inlaid with rubies and emeralds.   They showed no sign of wear and were worn only as ornaments.   In the work above mentioned it is stated that the swords of Persia are generally worn by the Indian Rajahs, and in the same spirit

37

the Nabobs of India secured the bejeweled thumb-rings from Persia to decorate the person. On the borders of Persia and Tartary the composite bow and the thumb-ring might have been introduced, but the aboriginal bow of India was the long bow. I have already shown that the Bhils and other aboriginal tribes of India practiced the Mediterranean release.

In the earliest records of India no allusion is made to the thumb-ring. PROF. E. WASHBURN HOPKINS, the author of a profound memoir on the Hindu Epic going back to Buddhistic times, writes me as follows: "In so far as I know about the matter the Hindu archer wore 'hand-guards' and 'finger-guards' (talatrana and anguitrana respectively) and the latter may have been in ring shape, but they are spoken of as made of iguana skin, not of metal. The warriors all wore 'finger-guards' as protection from the bow string. (*Jour. Am. Oriental Soc.*, Vol. XIII, pp. 304 and 308.) Rings are for seals, but metal rings for bow-men are not mentioned."

It is significant that the ancient people of India used finger-guards made of iguana skin, in other words, leather tips for the fingers, as used by all European archers today, and shows that these ancient people practiced the same release that is used by the aboriginal tribes of India at the present time.

Having appealed to Indian classics for information about the arrow release of the early people we turn to Chinese classics and find in the ancient writings of China indisputable evidences of the use of the thumb-ring. In the *Shi King*, or book of ancient Chinese poetry the following allusions are made to the use of the thumb-ring, which was also called a thimble, and a *pan chi*, or "finger regulator." "With archer's thimble at his girdle hung," and again "Each right thumb wore the metal guard."

In the Chinese Chrestomathy, translated by E. C. BRIDGMAN, the rules for archery gives, for the eyes: "Never look at the thumb-ring," and "The thumb-ring is made of ivory and fitted to the thumb of the right hand; by it the string is held and the bow bent." In these two records we learn that in ancient times these rings were made of metal

38

and ivory. From the above consideration I cannot find any evidence that archers' rings were made in India and those objects in European museums and in private collections labeled as such were probably made in Persia or in Turkey. HANSARD (p. 136) in a foot-note quotes another author as saying, "One of the early Turkish Sultans occupied his leisure in manufacturing these rings "distributing them as presents among his favorites and adds that the carnelian thumb-rings may be easily procured in the bazaars of Constantinople.

An invariable accompaniment of the Mongolian release is the thumb-ring. This may be made of bronze, iron, brass, ivory, deer-horn, jade, agate, carnelian and glass. There are two distinct types of thumb-rings; one type is cylindrical, long, thick, rarely ornamented. This type belongs strictly to China; the other type is shorter, oblate, never cylindrical, one side flaring and in profile resembling, more or less the visor of a cap. This type is found in Persia, Turkey, Asia Minor and Syria. The horn-ring of the Koreans belongs to this type, the flaring part being greatly elongated. The Persian rings of jade are occasionally inlaid with gold, or with emeralds and rubies, or, when of metal, with incised floral designs. The jade rings beautifully inlaid with gems show no signs of wear, they have never been used and were worn as ornaments to the person. In the same way the Japanese inro, or medicine box, of the Japanese, at first a simple and serviceable box for stomachics became finally a marvel of gold lacquer work and was worn as an ornament by Daimios and wealthy Samurai.

A very old ring of the flaring type was dug up by DR. FELIX VON LUSCHAN four hours out from Damascus, between that city and Palmyra. He graciously gave it to me remarking that it was an *unicum*. Having reason for believing that the Hittites used the Mongolian release and the region in which this was found coming well within Hittite territory, is it possible that this ring might prove to be a Hittite ring? The ring is of bronze and deeply worn and marks of a scroll design coarsely engraved is seen on its face, though nearly obliterated by wear, yet enough remains to show that the design is bi-symmetrical. My daughter, MRS. RUSSELL ROBB, endeavoured to interpret the intentions of

39

the artist, and the enlarged drawing here given with the ring (Fig. 33) is the result. If her interpretation is correct it may aid in ascertaining the age and provenance of the object.

Fig. 33   Ancient metal thumb ring Asia Minor

I am not able to find distinguishing differences between those rings marked Persia and those marked Turkey; it would seem, however, that the highly decorated ones were made in Persia when one considers the gorgeous swords with bejeweled handles known as Persian are worn by Indian Rajahs. In the illustrations to follow the orginal labeling will be preserved, bearing in mind, however, that those marked India were probably Persian in origin.

At the Royal Toxophilite Society of London, where I had the pleasure of shooting with MR. LONGMAN, I found in the collection of the society some archery implements presented by MUMFORD EFFENDI, Secretary of the Embassy, from the Sublime Porte in 1794. Among these objects was an ivory thumb-ring (Fig. 34). A curious leather flap issues from the base of the ring to prevent the string from slipping off the ring into the angle of the thumb formed by the bent joint. In the National Germanic Museum at Nuremberg there was a Turkish thumb-ring of ivory with a similar leather attachment. The date of this ring was marked 1683 (Fig. 35). The guide book of the Museum stated that the Turkish objects were secured at the raising of the seige of Vienna which had been taken by the Turks and retaken by German and Polish armies under the command of GENERAL JOHN SOBIESKY. A tent also in the collection belonged to the Grand Vizier KARA MUSTA-PHA. The bow was typically Mongolian. The arrow had four barbs and was beautifully made. It is interesting to observe that a time space of one hundred and eleven years separates the two rings above figured and yet the free border of the leather flaps are identical in shape. An ivory Turkish ring of a later date, in the collection of

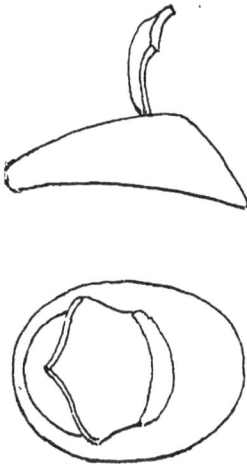

Fig. 34   Thumb ring Turkey   Fig. 35   Thumb ring Turkey

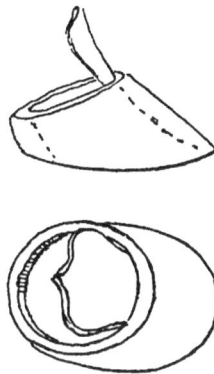

MR. GEORGE C. STONE, of New York city, has a leather edge cut squarely across (Fig. 36). In the case with these objects at the Nurem-burg Museum was a drawing showing the attitude of the hand in hold-ing the bow. A semi-tube of horn was grasped against the bow; a device made to enable the archer to pull the arrow within the bow in flight shooting, this was turned outward as if its purpose was to guide the arrow. The thumb-ring which should, of course, be on the right thumb is here shown on the thumb of the left hand upside down and backward! I informed the Director of the errors in the drawing and

41

mention it now for the purpose of showing how little attention had been paid to these minor details. As this was nearly thirty-five years ago these errors have probably long since been corrected.

While the Japanese practiced the Mongolian release I have never seen a thumb-ring, ancient or modern, in Japan. Instead of a ring they use a glove in which the thumb is greatly enlarged and grooved to admit the string. The glove may have the first and second fingers or all the fingers, the palm and back of the hand being uncovered. Mr. GEORGE C. STONE, to whom I am indebted for the privilege of drawing a number of archers' rings in his collection, in a letter to me, says, "I presume

Fig. 36   Thumb ring Turkey

you have a collection of archers' gloves with re-enforced thumbs, if not I have them with two and three fingers and one pair of full gloves. The latter are peculiar, the right thumb has an extra thickness of leather on the inside where the bow string would bear and the second and third fingers on both gloves are of a very much softer and lighter colored leather than the rest of the gloves. Both have ventilated openings in the palms." The Japanese archer's glove figured in the Badminton Archery is decorated with leaves on the thumb side. The Japanese archer's glove figured in my memoir represents the typical form in Japan.

In closing I wish to express my obligations to MR. LAWRENCE WATERS JENKINS for hunting up important references; to GEORGE C. STONE ESQ., of New York, for permission to figure a number of interesting archers' rings from his collection; to DR. W. P. WILSON,

42

Director of the Commerical Museum of Philadelphia, who while Chairman of the Philippine Government Board, St. Louis Exposition enabled me to study the Negritos from the Philippine Islands; to MR. KOJIRO TOMITA for translations of Chinese characters and to those whose names are mentioned in the pages who helped me in various ways without whose kind assistance this contribution to the subject could not have been made.

The following plates represent archers' rings drawn natural size, many of them hasty sketches. The first three plates are supposed to be Turkish and Persian rings, some of them attributed to India. MR. GEORGE C. STONE informs me that on his last visit to the South Kensington Museum he saw a collection of possibly fifteen jade rings inlaid with rubies and emeralds, labeled India. If made in India it would be interesting to find out precisely in what place in India they were made.

In the collections of the Boston Museum of Fine Arts is an archer's thumb-ring of green jade with incised floral design in gold and rubies, a band of gold encircling each ruby. It bears no sign of wear and must have been worn purely as an ornament for the hand. It is exquisite in its beauty and workmanship. See plate III, Fig. 5.

The last two plates represent archers' rings from China.

White Jade, Ethnological Museum, Leyden, Persia

43

APPENDIX

TRANSACTIONS OF THE BERLIN SOCIETY FOR ANTHROPOLOGY,
ETHNOLOGY AND PRIMEVAL HISTORY
Meeting of July 18, 1891

(P. 670. Paper on Bending the Bow. M. FELIX VON LUSCHAN).
(Figs. 10 and 12 are omitted in the following extracts)

After considering the primary, secondary, tertiary, Mediterranean and Mongolian methods of bending (drawing) the bow, and after considering a variety of arrangements for protecting fingers, hands and arms against a recoil of the bowstring the author returns (p. 674) to

Fig. 7

the Mongolian method with thumb ring in the right hand which it requires, he instances such rings from Syria, Korea and China and then says: It is very surprising that we should also have knowledge of such a ring in Africa. In the Royal Museum for Ethnology at Berlin there is an iron thumb ring (Fig. 7, p. 675) from the Benue country, collected by R. FLEGEL and designated by him as a bow-bending ring.

In the face of such a statement, even if so far it has remained an isolated one it cannot be doubted that the Mongolian method is known also in Africa, for it is only with this method that a thumb ring can occur. I, myself, have a small ring with a long lateral spur (projection) made of some light-colored oxidized metallic alloy which ERNST MARNO brought from the Giraffe River and designated as a ring for bending the bow (Fig. 8a). As MARNO could not at the time explain

44

to me how it was possible to bend a bow with such a ring, I took no further notice of his statement and considered the ring to be a knuckle-duster. But there is in the Berlin Museum, as I saw only recently, a horn ring shaped quite similarly only larger, which is also designated as a ring for bending the bow (Fig. 8b) Although the way of using the ring is not clear as yet, nevertheless this furnishes now, after twenty years, an entirely unexpected confirmation of MARNO's old statement and we will probably be constrained to assume also for the upper Nile regions the occurrence, an isolated occurrence perhaps, of the Mongolian method. The actual manner of using these thumb-

Fig. 8a   Fig. 8b

rings with lateral spur remains occult, just as it has to be made clear how in Korea this diverging form has there arisen and maintained itself, alongside of the form usual and typical there. Aside of the five above mentioned methods of bending the bow, MORSE enumerates a few others of less importance which are partly only individual methods and of which only one could be explained here, the bending with both hands. The archer lies on his back pressing both feet firmly against the bow. I, myself, have seen Bushmen shoot in this way, but the impression this made upon me was rather that of an artist's feat (an exhibition performance than that of a typical use.) On the other hand I am today in the position to communicate a hitherto entirely unknown method of bending the bow, *the Wute Method*. For the knowledge of it we are indebted to 1ST LIEUTENANT MORGEN, the dashing and lively successor of CAPTAIN KUND, who observed this method with the Wute people in the back country of Kamerun and brought several pieces as ocular demonstration to Berlin. Unlike all other people of whom we know so far the Wute bend the bow not at all with the fingers but with the middle of the hand. For this they

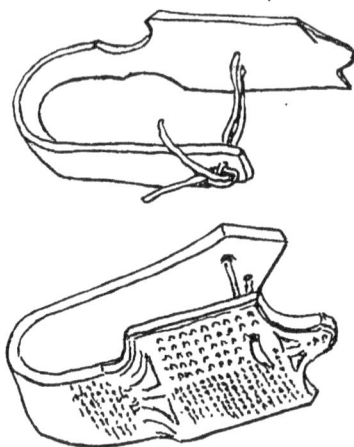

Fig. 9

use a ring which consists as Figure 9 shows of a small thin piece of board, bent like a bow (of a necktie) the ends of which may be drawn, more or less, together according to the size of the hand, by means of a leather thong (strip). This ring is worn in such a way that it is drawn over the hand to its middle with the closed end towards the radius and the open end towards the ulna. The string of the bow is caught and drawn tight with the edge of the radial side, whilst the thumb keeps the arrow in the desired position.

46

In succession to these hand rings follow, of course, the West African daggers with hollow handles (Figs. 10 and 11) which have so far become known to us (as existing) in the protectorate of Togo the Wute country and the Benue regions, especially (specifically) from the latter. STAUDINGER and HARTERT brought already, 1886, a long dagger knife (Fig. 10) of the kind which they found with the Kadarra and Korro tribes where these knives serve as well as a hand weapon for defense, as for the quicker bending of the bow, by pressing the handle against the string.

This statement is, of course, not quite clear, as with such aid one may gain rather in power, but hardly in quickness, nevertheless it results without dispute from this statement, that *de facto* also these tribes have the same manner of bending the bow, which since then

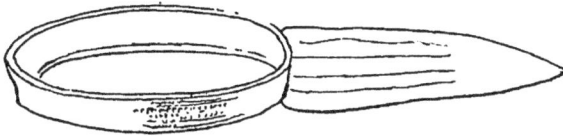

Fig. 11

has been recognized more distinctly a little farther south by LIEU-TENANT MORGEN. But the Berlin Ethnological Museum has very numerous specimens of quite similar knives from the Togo Protectorate brought thence by staff-physician DR. WOLF and by DR. BUTTNER and to the latter we are also indebted for the names Ssegara and Sama, both of which, as it seems, are common in the Sugu language, for the knives. It is true both travelers have considered them only as such (knives) and do not mention that they are also used for bending the bow, but there seems to be no doubt that they, just as the similar knives in the Benue countries, serve both purposes, at all events we have the specific information as regards the knife, (Fig. 11) from the Wute countries, that it is also used for bending the bow therefore besides the above described wooden middle-hard-rings,

47

which serve the same purpose. To examine which is here the original and which the derived forms would be a difficult and perhaps also a useless task, at all events already the above consideration shows —. and practical attempt confirms — that this method of bending the bow, whether by the aid of the wooden hand-ring, or by that of the iron dagger-handle, is an extremely powerful method. As a matter of fact it is far and away superior to every other method, not only on account of the ease with which the full strength of the whole arm is brought to bear upon the string, but also on account of the extraordinary delicacy with which the arrow is released at the decisive moment.

The enormously powerful effect produced by this (bending) ring finds its counterpart in a protective apparatus for the left hand, which exceeds in its dimensions everything existing before. It consists (Fig. 12) of a strip of leather tightly fitting the wrist, open and arranged for tying on the ulnar side, and carrying on the thumb side an irregularly conical erection of 10-15 cm. high also made of string or leather (hide) colored black and generally embellished with geometric ornamentations. This peculiar (or peculiarly) a symmetrical wrist band presents therefore to the rebounding string two inclined planes which completely paralyse even the hardest blow.

The pursuit of the subordinate (minor) and apparently unimportant inquiry as to the method of bending the bow used by different peoples results thus in the disclosing of an unexpected manifoldness (variety) and furnishes inducment in various directions for further reflection. The material collected so far contains, however, by far too many gaps if the above communication concerning the Wute method fills one of these in a manner so entirely *sui generis*, the other gaps appear only the more lamentable, I may, therefore, be allowed to express the hope that future travellers will pay more attention to this question than has been done hitherto, and that the excellent. observation of LIEUTENANT MORGEN will by no means remain the last one of its kind.

.

PLATE I

Figure 1 White jade, inlaid with rubies and emeralds. FRANKS' Coll. Attributed to India.

.2 White jade, deeply inlaid with gold. GEORGE C. STONE Coll. Persia.

3 Bronze; design roughly cut. FRANKS' Coll. Bought at Smyrna.

4 Thin brass, overlapping behind, design roughly cut. British Museum. No locality given.

5 White jade, inlaid with rubies and emeralds. FRANKS'. Coll. No locality given.

6 Iron, inlaid with copper and brass. British Museum., Persia.

PLATE I

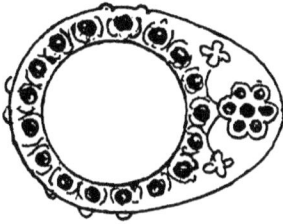

2

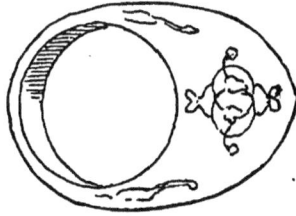

1

3

4

5

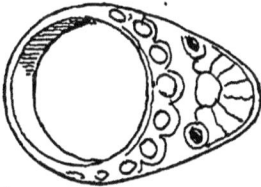

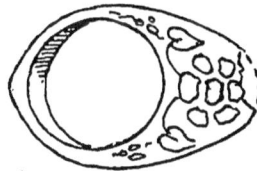

6

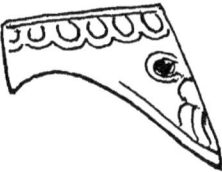

PLATE II

Figure 1 White jade, with floral design in slight relief. GEORGE C. STONE Coll. Persia. 17th century.

2 White jade. British Museum. Persia.

3 Bone. British Museum. Persia.

4 Carnelian. British Museum. Persia.

5 & 6 Carnelian. Ashmolean Museum, Oxford.
These are recorded in the old catalogue as follows:
"Tradescantianum, or Collection of Rarities preserved at South Lambert, near London, by JOHN TRADESCANT, London. MDCLVI."

PLATE II

1

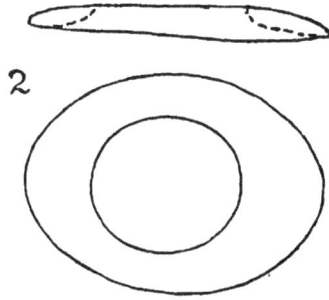

2

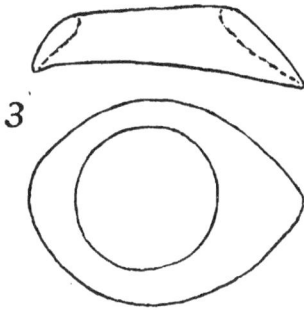

3

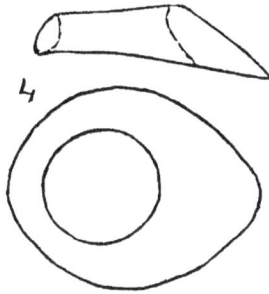

4

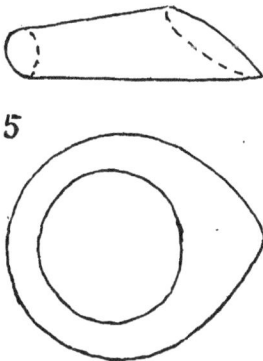

5

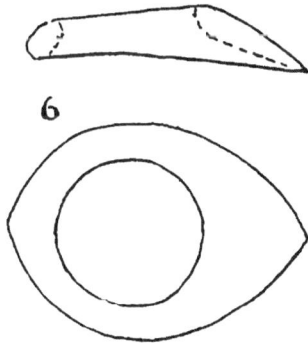

6

PLATE III

Figure 1 Bone, closely inlaid with minute bits of brass with a band of larger round bits of brass. FRANKS' Coll. Bought at Smyrna.

2 Bone. Failed to record nature of inlay. British Museum. Siberia?

3 White jade with slight keel on back. GEORGE C. STONE Coll.

4 Ivory, simple decoration of circles and leaves. GEORGE C. STONE Coll.

5 Green jade inlaid with gold and rubies. Boston Museum of Fine Arts.

6 White jade. GEORGE C. STONE Coll.

PLATE III

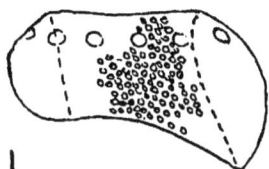

1

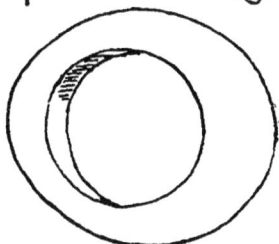

2

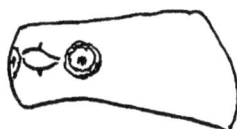

3

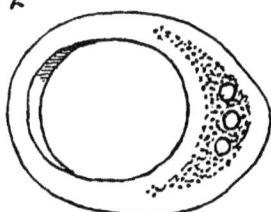

4

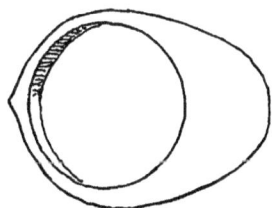

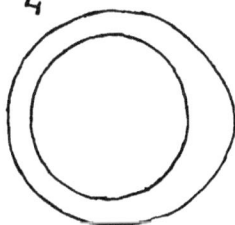

5

6

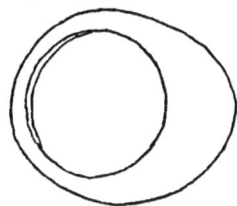

PLATE IV

Figure 1   Greenish variegated jade. Peabody Museum, Salem.

2   Deer horn. Peabody Museum, Salem.

3 and 4   Deer horn. From a group of five deer horn rings. GEO. C. STONE Coll. I have selected the largest and smallest to figure.

5   Ivory, with double character for "joy" in slight relief, GEO. C. STONE Coll.

6   Dark brown substance, "neither wood, metal or stone." Bamboo design, slightly etched, silver lined. GEO. C. STONE Coll.

7   Weathered jade, resembling jade from old tombs. GEO. C. STONE Coll.

8   Steatite. Peabody Museum, Salem.

9   Stone, characters in ancient form in slight relief. They read "Speak with sincerity." It is from the Analects of Confucius, Book I, Chap. 7. Peabody Museum, Salem.

10   Marble. Peabody Museum, Salem.

PLATE IV

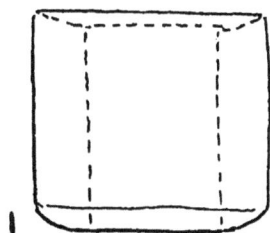

1

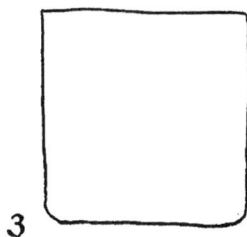

3

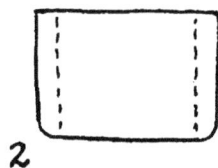

2

4

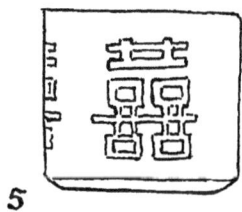

5

6

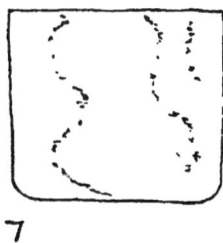

7

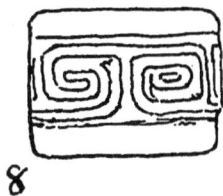

8

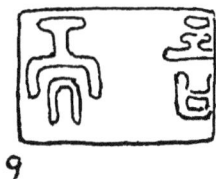

9

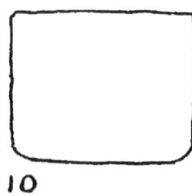

10

PLATE V

Figure 1 White jade, Hydra in slight relief, flattened on one side. FRANKS' Coll.

2 White jade, abruptly flattened on one side, landscape in slight relief. GEO. C. STONE Coll.

3 White jade, abruptly flattened on side, the flat portion somewhat discolored. The flattened side, from its appearance, represents the original surface of the block of jade from which it was made. GEO. C. STONE Coll.

4 Amber-colored glass, deep yellow. Abruptly flattened on one side; flattened side slightly curved. Peabody Museum, Salem.

PLATE V

1

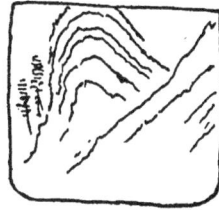

2

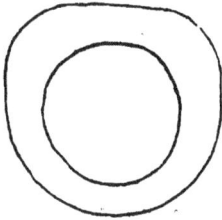

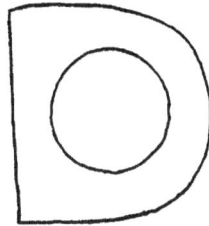

3

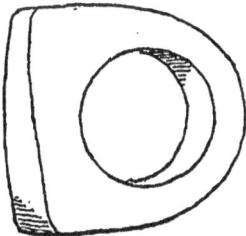

4

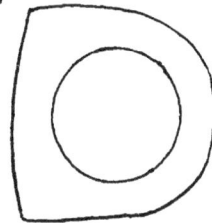

CPSIA information can be obtained
at www.ICGtesting.com
Printed in the USA
LVHW111347011118
595629LV00001B/252/P

9 781473 329164